MESSAGES
FROM ANGELS

An Hachette UK Company
www.hachette.co.uk

Material first published in *Advice From Angels* in Great Britain
in 2005 by Godsfield Press,
a division of Octopus Publishing Group Ltd
Carmelite House, 50 Victoria Embankment, London EC4Y 0DZ
www.octopusbooks.co.uk

This edition published in 2017 by Bounty Books, a division of
Octopus Publishing Group Ltd

ISBN 978-0-7537-3264-9

A CIP catalogue record for this book is available from the
British Library

Printed and bound in China

10 9 8 7 6 5 4 3 2 1

For the Bounty edition
Publisher: Lucy Pessell
Designer: Lisa Layton
Editor: Sarah Vaughan
Production Controller: Beata Kibil

MESSAGES FROM ANGELS

For comfort and reassurance

MESSAGES FROM ANGELS

For comfort and reassurance

CONTENTS

INTRODUCTION

Angels are beings of light. Messengers of God, angels are intermediaries between humankind and the Divine. Healers, protectors, bearers of information and joy, sources of inspiration, guardians and friends, they come to us in many ways and give advice and counsel that is both practical and uplifting.

Angels don't have to prove themselves. They just are.

Whoever you are, whatever your faith, and whether or not you believe these words, you have been given a wonderful gift – the love of angels.

Having accepted it with gratitude, you are asked to share it with others at every opportunity. All faiths instruct us to love one another. This teaching is not just a sugary sentiment; it asks you to act truly from the heart as angels do.

THE ROLE OF ANGELS

Angels in vast numbers are sent to Earth to help us in our humanness and assist our spiritual growth. Many people have already awakened to their call for realignment, attunement and enlightenment. When you tune in to the wonderful energy of angels, you are instantly aware of the love that emanates from their presence – a love that ignites a spark in the heart that can never be extinguished.

Never be misled by the use of the word love. There is no implication of 'softness' here. Being kind in action and thoughtful in a loving way does not make you a doormat. Angels are not soft and feathery. Appointed as our guides, guardians and protectors of justice, angels are the soldiers of Heaven!

Archangel Michael, Lord of the Archangels, is portrayed armed with a sword and bears God's holy armour. His role is to protect, and he is often shown slaying the dragon. A spiritual warrior and defender of right, he inspires us to cut away the dross in our own lives and defend truth as we venture along life's journey.

LOVING POWER

We can all act with power but in a loving manner.

It is mothering without smothering, being of service without the need to control or dominate.

Acting with love is acting as the angels would. If we all behaved like angels, Earth would be a lot more like Heaven!

By inviting the angels into our lives and receiving their guidance, we ignite the Divine spark within us – that part of us that is linked to the angels. Imagine the enthusiasm generated when we light that spark and they see it glowing and growing.

All we need is pureness of intention and a loving heart.

USING THIS BOOK

Whether or not you already work closely with the angelic forces, you will feel the energy of their love in this beautiful book.

Allow yourself to be inspired by the joy captured in these words of angelic wisdom.

Allow the spark of angelic love to be kindled in your heart and make your world a little more Heavenly. This book will inspire your thoughts, nourish your being, warm your heart and ignite the angelic spark within you.

It will lovingly remind you that you are never alone because there is always an angel by your side.

ANGEL-BEING

'UTOPIA WILL COME TO PASS ONLY
WHEN WE GROW WINGS AND ALL
PEOPLE ARE CONVERTED
TO ANGELS.'

FYODOR DOSTOEVSKY

The celestial beings are only one of the many aspects of Divine essence. God is everywhere.

As humans we are made up of the four elements – air, water, earth and fire – but we are powered by the energy of the Divine within. How can we believe that we are separate from God?

When there is joy in the world we celebrate as one. How can we not know that when one suffers, the whole consciousness of the Earth takes part in that pain?

When we pollute the rivers, when we cut down the trees, when we hunt down animals until they are extinct, can we not feel the universal sorrow?

You have the capacity for great healing and joy. The creativity and love of the angels combined with the ingenuity of human intellect can blend into a fine force. Recognize that power within you and dedicate it to the whole.

You will be amazed at the gifts that power will give you.

'I HAVE BEEN ON THE VERGE OF
BEING AN ANGEL ALL MY LIFE, BUT
IT HAS NEVER HAPPENED YET.'

MARK TWAIN

When you start to work with the angels you won't suddenly become a different person. You won't become unrecognizable, looking ten years younger or twenty pounds lighter, and all your worries will not miraculously fade away. You will have the same personality traits and probably the same aches and pains too!

Inviting the angels into your life simply allows you to connect with your real self, and reminds you who you really are. It will enable you to open your heart, connect with your soul, your higher self, your intuition and your companion angels.

Working with angels is not fluffy, happy-clappy, feel-good stuff. Far from it! You will become stronger, more focused, confident, compassionate, self-reliant, connected, centred and authentic. The changes are not necessarily physical... or are they?

DON'T WORRY IF YOU FALL ON YOUR
FACE WHILE LEARNING TO FLY –
PRACTICE MAKES PERFECT.

This is a time of consciousness raising, but also a time of consciousness crushing. We live in an age when spirituality is acknowledged as an essential part of life, and yet a life of spirituality is often ignored or ridiculed.

So what do you do when you have found your path of spiritual truth and you want to follow it?

Honour yourself, and practise. Practise by example, using humour, serenity, humility, kindness and sincerity.
You will be helped in your challenge, with your choices, and with directions.

The angels will work through synchronicity to send into your life the circumstances and people you need for support. You can do this; you can fly.

'THE MORE WE LOVE WHAT IS GOOD
AND TRUE, THE MORE THE ANGELS
LOVE TO BE WITH US.'

EMANUEL SWEDENBORG

The gift of life contains no promises, only possibilities.

We are called to live our lives with appropriate regard for others. We are interdependent with all things on our wonderful planet. If you sincerely immerse yourself in the service of others you cannot help but be helped yourself.

Rather than ask what you can get from life, ask: 'How may I serve? What can I contribute?'

Many blessings are around you everywhere, so don't miss the opportunity to make a difference.

WE ARE ALL ANGELS – IT'S WHAT WE DO WITH OUR WINGS THAT MAKES US DIFFERENT.

There was a forest fire and all the animals were fleeing for their lives, except for one humming-bird who was flying among the blossoms.

As a monkey went by in the tops of the trees he called to the hummingbird: 'Come on, you're going to burn, we all have to fly for our lives.' 'No, I can't,' said the little hummingbird as she visited another flower, filled her tiny beak with nectar and poured the drop of moisture on to the flames. She flew to the next flower to repeat the process. 'You must hurry,' chattered the monkey. 'You'll die if you don't come now.' 'Not at the moment,' said the hummingbird. 'But what are you doing?' asked the monkey impatiently. 'I am doing my bit,' said the hummingbird finally.

You don't have to be a great enlightened master to do your bit. It is how you do it that is important; it is your intention to serve the greater purpose.

GOD WANTS SPIRITUAL FRUITS NOT
RELIGIOUS NUTS!

Fanaticism and dogma are not enlightening. Is it not better to gently sow the seeds of wisdom and love into areas of strife, allowing them to grow in their own time?

You are on your own spiritual journey, and are always in the right place at the right time, even though the decisions you make may affect your progress at times.

Don't be afraid that someone else may seem 'more spiritual' than you.

Your light is just as bright; don't be afraid to let it shine.

There is nothing 'spiritual' or enlightening about imposing one's intellectual truth on someone else. All the great masters taught in simple parables and stories that made their teachings accessible to all levels of understanding.

How motivating and inspiring it can be to share ideas with like-minded people who are now harvesting the fruits of their own spiritual maturity.

THE KIND WORDS OF AN ANGEL MAY
BRIGHTEN THE HOUR AND LIGHTEN
THE DAY.

'I want you to know,' said the stranger, 'that you have helped me through my depression and my life is back on track, thanks to you.' 'Sorry, I don't know what you mean,' replied the young woman, wishing she had not answered the door. 'Well, every time I saw you walking down the street, you gave me a warm smile and passed the time of day with me. When you drove past in your car, you waved as if you knew me. Your smile brightened my day and lifted me somehow. You made me feel as if someone really cared. I just thought I'd find out where you lived so that I could tell you how grateful I am. It wasn't hard to find you. I just asked if anyone knew the young woman with an old "Beetle" car and a smile like an angel.'

A few kind words cost nothing but the effort.

ONCE YOU OPEN AND STRETCH
YOUR WINGS, YOU'LL SEE FEATHERS
EVERYWHERE.

Open your wings and be the angel that you can be.

Sit with your eyes closed, breathe deeply and relax; let go of any stresses and anxieties held in your body.

Visualize your guardian angel behind you with open hands poised over your shoulders.

Imagine the warmth of loving energy coming from those healing hands.

Visualize your angel placing an index finger on each of your vertebrae, down your spine.

Imagine you have two unused folded wings attached to your shoulder blades.

Ask your angel to open your wings.

Feel their wonderful strength and softness. The angel encases them in a divine radiance visible to all angels of light.

In gratitude, breathing deeply, bring yourself back into the moment.

Hold the sensation of becoming an angel and feel empowered to share love and joy in every situation.

THE ART OF AN ANGEL IS THE
HEART OF AN ANGEL.

How good are you at sharing with others? Most of us share friendship and fun together but how easy is it to share our private feelings?

Our thoughts, ideas and love, the reality of who we really are, these are often kept very close to our hearts for fear of rejection, ridicule, criticism and pain.

Sharing is a two-way living experience. The universal law of generosity works in such a way that what you give willingly will be returned to you, sometimes more fully.

Sit meditatively and create a safe space for yourself, then call upon the Angels of Harmony to draw close to you.

Ask them to help dissolve barriers of poverty-consciousness or rejection that prevent you from sharing either your material possessions or your feelings.

Surround yourself in a pink loving light of warmth and know that you are always supported in your generosity.

'BE NOT FORGETFUL TO ENTERTAIN
STRANGERS, FOR IN SO DOING
SOME HAVE ENTERTAINED ANGELS
UNAWARES.'

HEBREWS 13:2

Jo had been repelled by a tramp at the door asking for food. Wishing to be charitable, she brought him sandwiches and a drink.

There was something unnerving about the man's stare. His eyes were blue and piercing, yet gentle and 'all-knowing'. Spreading a rag on the grass he sat to eat and thanked her for her kindness.

After a few minutes he had gone leaving no sign, but a beautiful white feather floated on to the kitchen table.

ANGELIC
GUIDANCE

'ANY SORT OF PRETENCE SEEMS
UNWORTHY OF ANGELS.'

SAINT THOMAS AQUINAS

Often the decisions we make create self-imposed challenges, which are wonderful opportunities for spiritual growth. But, if we do not face the challenge, not only will we miss a chance to move on, we will have to face the same challenge over and over until we do confront it.

Be honest with yourself. If you deceive yourself by pretending that everything is perfect your goals become hazy, you bury your potential brilliance under layers of self-deception and illusion and you defeat your quest for self-improvement.

Ask the angels for help!

'IF YOU WANT TO TELL ANYTHING TO
GOD, TELL IT TO THE WIND.'

AFRICAN PROVERB

Listen to your inner being. Only in the stillness of the depths of the soul can you know God.

Find the small voice within. Everything you experience is remembered. Every answer is found within.

Only in the silence can the answers be heard. But sometimes this is forgotten and so we pray out loud to articulate our fear or despair, or to plead for guidance.

When you speak out you affirm your thoughts to the Universe. You sense them through hearing the words as well as thinking and feeling them.

If you talk to your angels, the messages are carried directly to God.

If you pray directly to God the angels respond immediately.

Voice your prayers out loud to the Universe, choose your words carefully, open your heart... the angels are there.

'OUTSIDE THE DOORS OF STUDY. . .
AN ANGEL AWAITS.'

HANNAH GREEN

Sometimes, in striving to do our best, we become so obsessed with work or study that we forget we are spiritual beings in human form.

Our journey is to bring knowledge gained into our spiritual life and our spirituality into everyday life.

We become so wrapped up in our personal agenda that we often forget that life is not meant to be difficult. Challenging, perhaps, but smoother than most of us realize.

Ask Archangel Gabriel and God's Angels of Wisdom to guide you with love back on to your spiritual path.

'THE EARTH IS TO THE SUN WHAT
MANKIND IS TO THE ANGELS.'

VICTOR HUGO

Without the sun the Earth would perish. Imagine the Earth without sunlight, without heat. Nothing would live. Humanity could not survive without light, but what of spiritual light? How do we illuminate the soul?

Archangel Jophiel and the Angels of Illumination are there to enlighten your spiritual pathway. In all aspects of creativity you can call for Jophiel's assistance.

Begin by lighting a candle and sitting quietly. Imagine you are surrounded by an infusion of clear golden-yellow light glowing around you.

Call to Jophiel and the Angels of Illumination and visualize them encircling you with their loving light energy.

As you breathe in, flood your whole body with this light.

Imagine yourself drawing in clarity, creativity and inspiration.

With every out-breath see density, confusion, darkness and discouragement dissolved by the angels' golden light.

DON'T BE AFRAID OF THE DARK,
IT IS ONLY THE LIGHT CASTING
SHADOWS.

It has been said that the brighter we shine, the more shadow we create. Sometimes these are the shadows within ourselves, those darker areas that we may not want to know about.

Becoming spiritually aware means facing those inner demons, confronting them with gratitude, dealing with them and moving on. If we wish to commit to change, then we have help readily available.

Sit quietly and, as you relax with your eyes closed, breathe deeply and let go of any tension in your body with each exhalation.

Invite your angel to stand by your side.

Imagine a blank screen in front of you.

Ask the angel to show you aspects of yourself that need work and watch the screen.

You may see a full image rather like a dream, or simple objects; you may hear music or words or experience a certain feeling.

WHAT SEEMS LIKE DEATH TO A
CATERPILLAR IS THE BIRTH OF A
BEAUTIFUL BUTTERFLY TO THE
MASTER.

What a fantasy – to feast to our heart's content, wrap ourselves in a warm cocoon, fall into a deep sleep and wake up to find ourselves transformed into a being of delicate beauty with wings to fly wherever we choose. Nothing is really that simple.

Firstly, the earthbound caterpillar is driven by need, insatiable hunger. It is not free until it has changed from this caterpillar phase.

If we are prepared to completely change from our insatiable 'needs' we are all capable of metamorphosizing into beautiful beings of light. It is through really letting go of your old self, and dying metaphorically, that the new you can come truly into the light.

This is what Jesus meant when he said we must all be born again.

SOMETIMES THE ANGEL'S GIFT IS
NOT TO GIVE YOU WHAT YOU WANT.

To want is an expression of need. It tells the Universe that there is a lack, a void, a wanting within us.

Remember the old adage given to demanding children: 'I want never gets'? Imagine constantly telling the Universe 'I want more' – negatively affirming that you are in a permanent state of lack! Better to create affirmations that reinforce what is already yours.

Instead of saying 'I want to be slimmer' or 'I wish I felt good', say 'My body grows more youthful every day and all my cells work in perfect harmony'.

Instead of saying 'I can't afford so-and-so', say 'I live in abundance, I always have enough'.

Notice the difference when you change 'I want someone to love me' to 'I am lovable and I attract loving people into my life'.

SHARE YOUR SECRET DREAMS WITH
THE ANGELS AND WATCH AS THEY
ALL COME TRUE.

It is said that the angels already know the higher plan for our lives. They sense our hopes and dreams, but cannot interfere with our human choices. This would be interfering with the laws of karma.

We are given circumstances where choices can be made, but as humans we often make this difficult for ourselves.

When petitioning the angels remember that intention and interpretation are important.

Angels are not like a 'genie of the lamp'; they don't fulfil your every desire. But wherever possible, and if your wish is for the highest possible good of all concerned, it is likely that you will have a favourable outcome.

'SOME PEOPLE REALLY SEE ANGELS
WHERE OTHERS SEE AN EMPTY
SPACE.'

JOHN RUSKIN

There are a few guidelines when you start to tune in to your angels and want to see them. Don't try too hard; just allow the vision to appear.

Be prepared to be surprised. Try not to hold on to preconceived ideas of what you will see or hope to see.

Some people see sparkling lights; others smell a wonderful fragrance, yet see nothing. Many see a bright light and occasionally an outline of a form.

Thousands of people have experienced angelic encounters of help or reassurances by a stranger, who then disappears, particularly in hospitals or during accidents.

It is more common to see nothing yet be aware of a calming, loving presence. Allow yourself to believe. Your prayers will be answered.

'THE ANGEL'S INTELLIGENCE IS
ALIGHT WITH THE PENETRATING
SIMPLICITY OF DIVINE CONCEPTS.'

DIONYSIUS

It is not surprising that our lives are full of confusion. By piling on the pressure, we create turmoil and disharmony.

Sit back for a moment and consider which of today's tasks are truly essential. If you do not complete them will the moon refuse to shine?

It is the ego that insists on cramming all this non-essential clutter into our lives – the fear of failure, the fear of rejection.

Give this day's tasks over in your mind to the angels and to God. Ask for the clarity of purpose of the Divine plan for your life. Ask that all your decisions and actions today are for the greater good of your higher consciousness, and for the highest good of all concerned.

As you clarify your actions and prioritize your day to the highest purpose, the angels will have the opportunity to guide and assist.

Keep it simple, concentrate your Divine light and watch your plan unfold.

ANGEL REASSURANCE

'AN ANGEL IS LIKE A MIRROR THAT REFLECTS THE TRUTH KINDLY, FOR IN ITS REFLECTION YOU CAN SEE WHO YOU TRULY ARE.'

ANTHEA CHURCH

Have you noticed how many different masks you wear? By developing a mask for every occasion you are pretending to be someone else.

Have you forgotten who you really are? You dilute your own energies, your personal magnetism and diminish your potential for growth by ignoring your true self.

Be courageous. Acknowledge your true self every day. Affirm your ability to be true to yourself. Call on your guardian angel and ask to be given the courage and honesty to be who you truly are.

'THE THOUGHTS AND ACTIONS OF
ANGELS ARE NOT LIMITED BY TIME
AND SPACE.'

EMANUEL SWEDENBORG

Angels are not tied to our three-dimensional reality. They have no concept of time and space, moving freely between our world and theirs.

An angel's movement is as quick as a thought. The great archangels can be in several places at any given time.

Don't be afraid that your personal dilemma is too insignificant to lay before an archangel, or that you will not be heard.

There are major catastrophes in the world and these need great shifts of understanding and human intervention. These are overseen by archangels at every given moment, but so are you.

The archangels can do both. The energetic loving energy they emit is beyond our human understanding.

A true request, for the right reasons, is never too simple nor too small to be heard by the angels.

You are loved and important. Never forget that.

ANGELS ARE THERE TO NOURISH
OUR BEING, NOT TO FEED OUR EGOS.

A hundred years ago almost everyone believed in God.
Every nation had a form of religious belief that was part
of its culture. Now most countries are known politically
as secular societies.

Yet human beings require nurturing of mind, body
and spirit. People are hungry to fulfil a yearning to
be complete.

The angels can help us. Truly ecumenical, angels act as a
link between God and us, as messengers, conveying our
thoughts and prayers to the source.

On the returning impulse of loving energy they prompt and
guide us in our thoughts and dreams.

This enables our spiritual growth through love so that we
begin to understand how precious we truly are.

AN ANGEL MAY SAVE THE DAY AND
SOMETIMES YOUR WHOLE LIFE.

Annie was in a devastating relationship. She desperately needed to leave with her children and start afresh.

As she sat at the bus stop a stranger sat down next to her and told her that she would find the courage she needed to change her life. The stranger then got up and walked away, without waiting for the bus to arrive.

Feeling puzzled by the potency of the stranger's words, Annie felt inspired, reassured and motivated. She packed and left for safety that weekend, and never looked back.

ONLY FEAR STOPS YOU FROM FLYING,
SO SPREAD YOUR WINGS AND ENJOY
THE RUSH!

What prevents us from reaching the top of the ladder?

What stops us from allowing ourselves to go with the flow, fly with the breeze?

The answer is our fear of failure. Yet the message of the angels is clear: there is no such thing as failure. Each time we try to fly, successfully or not, we learn and grow.

Believe in yourself as the angels do.

Believe in your ability to know instinctively that whatever you are doing with honest intention is always right.

Go ahead and trust yourself.

True happiness is allowing yourself to be who you really are.

ANGELS ARE ALWAYS THERE, EVEN
WHEN YOU THINK THE REST OF THE
WORLD HAS GONE AWAY.

We are never alone.

When we feel sad, lonely and even unloved, we need to remember that each of us has a guardian angel who knows and loves us even though no one else seems to care.

In a quiet peaceful place it is possible to think things through with your guardian angel who already knows all your problems and secrets.

Talk out loud to your angels and ask for a sign that is meaningful to you.

Practise listening and feeling as a form of meditation; this will bring the presence of the angels closer to you until a sense of 'knowing' is developed as a form of communication between you and your angels.

Feathers are a Divine symbol that your angels are with you.

'ANGELS MAY NOT ALWAYS COME
WHEN YOU CALL THEM, BUT THEY
WILL COME WHEN YOU NEED THEM.'

KAREN GOLDMAN

Like demanding children we can ask too much of the
angels, and develop a sense of lazy expectancy, relying on
someone else to do things for us.

Listen to your inner being. Find the still small voice within.

Everything we have ever experienced we remember deep in
our bodies; our memory is not just in the brain, but also in
our very cells.

We are capable of helping ourselves because we often do
know the answers.

It is important not to trivialize the angelic realms by
becoming dependent and petitioning angels for help with
every little thing in life.

When you are truly in need, when your heart and soul seek
ardently, you will find angels lovingly by your side showing
you the way.

ONCE AN ANGEL HAS TOUCHED YOU,
YOU WILL NEVER BE THE
SAME AGAIN.

Are angels imaginary?

The imagination is the creative expression of everything we know. Every experience is stored away in our soul memory. Certain thoughts, dreams or words can stimulate the creative aspect in our memory that triggers a vision in our mind's eye.

Angels present themselves in a manner that is acceptable to each individual.

When you hear an angel speak to you, or feel the loving wisdom touch your heart, when you stand in the presence of your guardian angel, whether in your dreams or physical reality, not only will you never forget, but your life will never be the same again.

'FOR AN ANGEL A MINUTE CAN BE
A THOUSAND YEARS, FOR TIME TO
ANGELS IS MEASURED IN LOVE.'

ANTHEA CHURCH

Have you lived your life dashing here and there fretting about being late?

This man-made phenomenon 'time' is a concept of little significance to the celestial realms. A moment of our time may as well be a thousand years.

If we are on a spiritual journey we may be amazed at the speed of our development. We start to fly with the angels. But, to our disappointment, we slide back into our normal routine for a while, feeling that perhaps we are forgotten.

You cannot be in a 'peak experience' all the time. If you fly near the sun too often, you will soon burn your wings. Your angels are still there; no more than a fleeting moment has passed in their terms. Their patience is immeasurable; after all, they may have been waiting for you all your life!

HUMANS MUST BE KNOWN TO BE
LOVED, ANGELS MUST BE LOVED TO
BE KNOWN.

When we love and are being loved our souls sing. We are
nourished and whole.

Loving others is easy, but in order to love unconditionally
we must first learn to love ourselves.

Loving is an expression of kindness, of communicating from
the heart and of compassion. Learn to give the gift of love
to yourself.

Think of a quality you deeply admire, one you would
attribute to an angel. Visualize that quality in the form of
a flower bud and in your imagination carry it to your very
core. Now look at the flower and admire it, appreciate
its perfection.

Remembering those qualities, recognize that you, too,
have these attributes. Acknowledge and respect yourself
for that.

Recognizing that your soul contains perfection, allow
yourself to love it. Your soul has the qualities of an angel.

As you begin to know yourself, you will learn how to
love yourself.

ANGELS IN ACTION

FRIENDS ARE ANGELS WHO LIFT OUR
FEET WHEN OUR OWN WINGS HAVE
FORGOTTEN HOW TO FLY.

A young child was brought into the hospital on a stretcher. She was unconscious and accompanied by her parents and a policeman.

Lucy had run into the middle of a very busy road where a truck had hit her and run over her twice. She was examined and only a small bruise on her shoulder was found.

Just before being sent for X-rays she opened her eyes and smiled.'Where is the man in white?' she demanded. The doctor came forward. 'No, no, the man in the long white, shiny dress.'

As her mother stroked her face, Lucy said, 'That man stroked my face as he picked up the wheels.'

WHEN YOUR LIGHT IS SHINING AT ITS
BRIGHTEST, BEWARE OF ATTRACTING
TOO MANY MOTHS.

When we open ourselves psychically we can be susceptible to interference from beings that are not necessarily useful to us.

It is very important to learn how to protect yourself. Primarily, call on Archangel Michael for protection and imagine an instant blue light surrounding you. Visualize a cloak of blue wrapped around you and request the protection of Michael's sword.

You can visualize yourself in a strong white light, like a spotlight, that is with you all the time.

If you wish, circle yourself with a golden light and ask that it protect you with Universal love and light.

Choose whichever method feels right for you and make a determined effort to establish it as one of your daily spiritual practices.

At the same time ask for the gift of discernment, that the angels will guide you to only what is right and true for the highest possible good of all concerned.

YOU CAN SEE THE LOVE OF ANGELS
REFLECTED IN THE FACES OF
SLEEPING CHILDREN.

There is a theory that many children being born now are old souls with highly developed spiritual skills. These very special children will remind us of long-forgotten healing techniques, psychic awareness and immeasurable compassion.

A beautiful story came to me recently.

A young mother became very worried by her five-year-old son's obsession with wanting to be left on his own with the new baby.

She stood quietly outside the bedroom door and allowed him to put his little sister into her crib.

Slightly fearful, she closed the door when he asked her to 'go away' but remained listening and ready to run into the bedroom.

Tears rolled down her cheeks when, to her surprise, he kissed his little sister and said:'Please help me to remember what it was like. I've forgotten already.'

AN ANGEL WILL NEVER GIVE UP ON YOU, EVEN IF YOU HAVE GIVEN UP ON YOURSELF!

Many of us are plagued by feelings of unworthiness or low self esteem.

Keep in mind that all thoughts create energy, and like attracts like. When we focus on negative thinking, we attract disappointments and disasters.

Archangel Chamuel and the Angels of Love can help you overcome negative feelings if you ask.

Close your eyes and ask that angelic love surround you.

Banish negative thinking by saying, three times, 'Be gone feelings of anti-love!'

See yourself surrounded by bright pink light and feel instantly uplifted.

Remember, also, that your guardian angels are with you even when you are feeling negative. You are special to your angels no matter how you are feeling about yourself.

Whenever you need reassurance, guidance, protection and love, just call on them for help. Soon you will be shown the way to happiness again.

ANGELS DON'T ALWAYS BLOW THEIR
OWN TRUMPETS – THE NOISE WOULD
BE DEAFENING!

There is no need to list all the wonderful things that angels do. Similarly, there is no need to tell the world how wonderful you are when you do something wonderful for someone else.

Spontaneous acts of kindness need no fanfare. The person receiving your generosity of spirit knows what you have done, as do the angels. Nothing is missed.

Archangel Metatron and the Recording Angels collect every thought and action in the Akashic Records – that cosmic storehouse of doers and deeds.

When you do something wonderful, Metatron takes note. Yet keep in mind that the kindest acts are those we do without expecting recognition.

TREAT EVERYONE YOU MEET WITH
LOVE – THEY MAY BE ANGELS IN
DISGUISE.

Angels and Ascended Masters are able to manifest in different forms. Very often the guise chosen is not what you would expect; remember that angels are non-denominational and the pictures we may have of blond, blue-eyed angels are our own imagination too.

I have heard of angels appearing as beggars, blind old men, little old ladies, tall Rastafarians, even angelic truck-drivers.

Angels are always around to help us when we really need them, but do we always feel the same way? By treating everyone as you like to be treated, by showing kindness at every opportunity, you too are spreading unconditional angelic love in action.

AS YOU KINDLE THE SPARK OF
ANGELIC LIGHT WITHIN YOUR HEART,
NOTICE THE GLOW IN OTHERS.

Once you light the spark of Divinity in your own heart you will feel a joy that you may not have experienced before. Your attitude to life may change and the world may seem a more beautiful place.

As you act towards others with love and notice how they respond with warmth to you, you will attract more loving people around you.

Imagine a spark of golden light glowing in your heart.

Close your eyes and visualize this loving angelic spark spreading its warmth and love through your chest.

As you breathe deeply, imagine this warm glow filling your whole body, legs, feet, arms, hands and through your neck and throat into your head.

Imagine that this wonderful loving light spreads out of your pores, glowing all over your skin.

Now imagine you can ignite the spark in others, simply with a loving smile – watch as this wonderful feeling spreads.

YOUR ANGELS ARE NOT THERE TO
JUDGE YOU, ONLY TO LOVE YOU.

You are the harshest judge of your own behaviour. Once you make a decision to work at areas in your life that may need some adjustment, ask the angels to help you soften your negative self-judgement with love.

Ask Archangel Zadkiel to help you to dissolve painful memories, to let go of judgement of self and others, and to enhance the spiritual gifts of forgiveness, tolerance and mercy.

Visualize yourself surrounded by a warm healing violet light that cleanses and purifies negative traits and painful memories that affect your dealings with others.

Allow yourself to bathe in this wonderful energy and feel refreshed and renewed.

'CHILDREN BELIEVE IN ANGELS AND
THE FEELINGS ARE MUTUAL.'

KAREN GOLDMAN

Ben, aged four, had been very sad since his Daddy had gone away. He hadn't eaten well, couldn't sleep and refused to play with his toys.

His mother Sue was beside herself with worry for her son and herself, but had read about the help of angels and came to see me to find out more.

In the week prior to her consultation, Ben came down from his room one evening after he had been put to bed and said: 'Mummy, there is a shiny lady in my room all dressed in white who knows who I am. I don't know what she wants but she keeps smiling and talking to me. Mummy, she is SO beautiful.'

Following the visit of the 'beautiful white lady', Ben became his normal happy self again, playing, eating and sleeping like a healthy little boy.

Do we need to return to innocence to see the angels for ourselves?

AN ANGEL'S GREATEST GIFT IS
PRESENCE IN THE PRESENT.

Isn't it strange how we are often unhappy no matter what we already have? Materially, we desire the lifestyles of others, their wealth or possessions, which we think will make our lives better.

Buddha taught that this attachment to wanting is what creates human suffering.

Remember that the past has already gone and is now history. The future is unknown and remains a mystery. That is why the gift is in the present.

Sit quietly and draw your attention to nothing but your breathing. As you breathe in deeply and then exhale, feel the air on the inside of your nostrils.

Don't think of anything else but the air and your slow breathing in and out. Do this for five minutes at first, gradually increasing to fifteen minutes.

By practising regularly you will develop the Zen technique of being 'in the now'. Enjoy your present!

ANGELIC CONNECTIONS

OUR DEEDS FASHION OUR DESTINY.
HEAVEN AND HELL ARE IN OUR
OWN HANDS.

Heaven is the divine connection to unconditional love and Hell is our fear of separation from it.

When we think, act and live with love, all is harmonious.

When we think, act and live in fear, then everything is surrounded by disharmony and difficulty.

Sit for a moment and breathe deeply. Imagine that you are inhaling a wonderful pink mist that is swirling all around you.

As you inhale, breath the pink mist into your entire body, and as you exhale let go of all your worries and tensions.

Affirm that you are totally supported by the Universe.

Call to Archangel Michael, thank him for his protection and ask that all fear be removed from your thoughts, that you may live in complete harmony with all aspects of life.

YOUR ANGELS DON'T SEE YOUR
PHYSICAL ACTIONS AND DEEDS,
ONLY THE INTENTIONS IN
YOUR MIND.

Angels are working in accordance with Divine law. Their only interest is to assist humanity to evolve into the light.

In Buddhism there is a belief that each of us has a 'Buddha-nature' that is capable of attaining Nirvana, or enlightenment, for ourselves.

One of the methods of finding our pathway to the light is that of 'right intention'; the idea is that it is not so much the action you take but the thought behind it. In your heart you are aware of your actions, and that you must hold the intention to do no harm.

Some who have reached enlightenment have developed such immeasurable compassion that they choose to remain as Bodhisattvas to help us on that path.

This is like the work of the archangels and great Ascended Masters who strive with us on many levels, lovingly guiding our route to union with the Divine, if that is our choice.

ANGELS KNOW YOU ARE USER-FRIENDLY, THEY SIMPLY FOLLOW THE MAKER'S INSTRUCTIONS PRINTED IN YOUR HEART.

I spent many years struggling with a feeling that there was something I was meant to be doing. Being a mother was wonderful, but that wasn't it. My nursing career was rewarding and fulfilling, but still wasn't it.

I began searching everywhere for answers, but still couldn't establish my true purpose in life.

Then I decided to pray ardently, offering myself in service knowing that, when I really meant it and was ready, the signs would appear.

I finally saw a course in 'healing with the angels' and signed up.

My guide told me: 'Welcome Christine, we've been expecting you. Your work will be arduous but we are here to support and guide you.'

Each of us has a soul purpose, a destiny to fulfil. The angels know it, they see the plan in our DNA and they are waiting for us to decide to go ahead.

AN ANGEL MAY REACH FOR YOUR
HAND AND TOUCH YOUR HEART.

There is a saying that 'once you hit the bottom the only way left is up'.

Many of us have felt the emptiness of despair. Whether caused by depression, bankruptcy, isolation, abandonment, abuse (self or other), alcohol or drugs, despair is like falling into a deep hole. It is at this point many of us turn to God.

When the soul cries out for help it is never denied. Angels respond immediately to your call. They will take your hand if you wish and pull you from the pit. This may happen physically, emotionally or mentally.

The overwhelming sense of love, well-being and gratitude this creates in your heart can hardly be described. Even better is the fact that, once you have experienced it, the memory will never leave you.

IF YOU WANT TO KNOW WHERE
HEAVEN IS, STOP LOOKING AT
YOUR FEET!

Have you noticed how we shuffle along with our shoulders hunched as if we carried the weight of the world on our backs?

With our eyes focused on the ground in front of us, we miss much of the beauty around us.

In the angelic hierarchy, nature Devas and spirits are as important as the rest. We connect with these beings by practising awareness of the beauties in nature.

Look up. Don't miss the butterfly flirting with the breeze, or the sparkling dew on the spider's web. Watch the speed and grace of the clouds racing across the sky.

When you see the wonders of nature, send these angels thoughts of gratitude and appreciation for the manifold beauties of this Heavenly world.

The next time you lean against a tree, ask a question from your heart. The answer will come from that sense of calm from the essence of the tree – from the angel that is its vital spirit.

WHEN YOU LOOK AT LIFE
THROUGH THE EYES OF AN ANGEL,
EVERYTHING IS IN GLOWING COLOUR.

Have you ever looked at the leaves on a tree as they turn in the breeze and noticed the intricacy of their form?

Have you noticed that the flowers adorning the chestnut are like tiny orchids when you examine them individually?

Have you stood recently and watched the sunset?

When you consider every particle of God's creation in its fine detail, and really see the beauty in everything, you are seeing life as it is truly meant to be seen.

When you begin to see through the eyes of an angel you cease judging others from a human perspective.

Every situation, every encounter, everyone you meet has an inner beauty. Life takes on a brighter hue that is always visible through the loving angelic eyes.

THE AIR SUPPORTING THE WINGS
OF AN ANGEL IS THE BREATH OF A
WHISPER OF GOD'S LOVE.

At the centre of all creation is love – in the rain, the earth, the petal of a flower, the fur of a kitten, the wing of a bee.

Love is in the sleeping face of a child, the song of a blackbird, the twinkling of a star.

Love is in the roar of the ocean as it crashes on to the shore, the delicate intricacy of a snowflake, the lightness of a feather.

Love is in the whisper, the whistle, the rustle, the rush, the strength and the power of the wind. The same wind that fuels a tornado also gently caresses your face in the breeze.

The wind that carries messages of fortune or disaster is the same wind that gives support beneath the wings of an angel. Your wings too.

AN ANGEL'S KINDNESS IS AN ACT OF
WORSHIP.

There are said to be nine choirs of angels.

Archangels represent the different aspects of the nature of God while at the same time adoring their Creator.

At the top of the hierarchy are the Seraphim who spend all their time singing in glory to God.

Divine loving energy cascades through the tiers of angels down to those who are closer to us.

Those angels at the lower end of the hierarchy are also working through, with and in honour of Divine love.

Everything they do for us is an act of worship. As this continuing, circulating angelic energy that passes down to us is worship, so too is every kindness that we perform on impulse without expecting a reward, given unconditionally and truly from the heart.

'IF YOU SEE THE ANGEL IN
EVERYONE YOU MEET, YOU WILL
ALWAYS BE IN DIVINE COMPANY.'

KAREN GOLDMAN

If our souls are everlasting, through many lifetimes, and if we wait in a heavenly place until our rebirth, then we spend most of that time among the angelic realms.

Following this thought, perhaps what we see in meditation is a memory. A part of us knows that angelic presence, and a spark of it remains in our hearts for all time.

When we are born, part of our soul – the ego-less, non-physical part – remains in the Heavenly place. The higher self is wiser and purer than our bodily form and has no material attachment.

It is possible to connect and ask our higher self for guidance. When we tap into that wisdom we can also connect with the angel within us.

Next time you meet, notice the difference in the energy of your interaction when you allow the angel within to connect with another at a deep soul level.

BEYOND THE VISIBLE SOFTNESS
OF AN ANGEL IS A FORCE OF
PURITY THAT THE WORLD CAN
NEVER BREAK.

This force is in the very softness of the dawn sky.

It can be sensed in the distant twinkle of stars.

It can be felt underfoot on a mossy riverbank, in the soft yielding of a white sandy beach.

It can be stroked in the softness of a child's hair. It is in the intricate feather left behind as a message from the angels.

It is in the filtered sunlight through the canopy of trees.

It is in the promise of the rainbow.

Yet its strength supports with the salty buoyancy of the ocean and the unbreakable pull of magnetic polarity.

It supports the hardness of rock, the very substance of our planet, refined through time. Seemingly fragile yet containing the unbreakable and everlasting promise that is contained in angelic protection and love.

GLOSSARY OF ARCHANGELS

Archangel Michael, Lord of the Archangels
A spiritual warrior and defender of right, Michael will help to protect you on your spiritual path.

Archangel Gabriel
A hero and messenger, Archangel Gabriel will guide you with love and gentle advice.

Archangel Jophiel
There to enlighten your spiritual pathway, Archangel Jophiel will assist you in all aspects of creativity within your spiritual journey.

Archangel Chamuel
An archangel of love and peaceful relationships, Archangel Chamuel can help you overcome negative feelings, if you ask.

Archangel Metatron
Collecting every thought and action for the Akashic Records – a collection of all human activity – you can be assured even your unrecognized deeds on Earth are seen and recorded by Archangel Metatron.

Archangel Zadkiel
To help you to heal painful memories, Archangel Zadkiel enhances the spiritual gifts of your ability to forgive and exercise tolerance and mercy.